IN A COUNTRY NONE OF US CALLED HOME

For Jilly —
Read 'em and
weep...
At least that's
what I did.
Hope some of these are
as personal for you
as they are for me.

David
6/6/14

IN A COUNTRY
NONE OF US
CALLED HOME

Poems

Peg Bresnahan

Press 53
Winston-Salem

Press 53, LLC
PO Box 30314
Winston-Salem, NC 27130

First Edition

Cover design by Kevin Morgan Watson

Cover art, "Flowers on a Chair," Copyright © 2007
by Ivan Ivanov, licensed thrugh iStock.

Printed on acid-free paper
ISBN 978-1-941209-01-1

For Dan

Acknowledgments

The following poems were first published, and may have appeared in slightly different versions, in the following journals, magazines and anthologies.

Baybury Review, "Paranormal"

Clothes Lines from 75 Western North Carolina Women, "Meltdown"

The Dead Mule School of Southern Literature, "Rescue Dog," "Visiting a Member of the Cedar Mountain Smuckers Club," "At the Sweet Hollow Baptist Church," "A Very Small Disaster in the Scheme of Things"

Free Verse, "Figuring Out Great-Grandmother Charlotte from Nothing but a Photograph"

Great Smokies Review, "Trigger"

Innisfree, "Water Witch"

KaKaLak, "After Attending an Exhibit of Henry Moore's Drawings and Sculpture," "Friday Night at Mike's"

Limestone, "Slipstream"

The Main Street Rag, "After I Played Tic-Tac-Toe with a Chicken," "Mary Alice Tries to Save the World"

Motif, "Instructions on Divination at the Old Cemetery"

The Nebraska Review, "Driving Back from Mt. Holy Cross"

The South Carolina Review, "Moscow, 1975"

Southern Poetry Review, "Living with Hephaestus"

Wisconsin Academy of Sciences and Arts/Bar Code, "In Willie's There's a Stool for Everyone"

Wisconsin Review, "Sometimes It Is Easier to Meet a Person in the Dark "

2012 Press 53 Open Awards Anthology, "At the Cemetery in Green Bay," "At the Sunny Ridge Retirement Center," "A Khmer's Scarf of One Thousand Functions"

2013 Press 53 Open Awards Anthology, "Radium Girls, 1924," "Decoding My Mother's Ledger from July 20, 1940," "That Space We Share"

Wisconsin Fellowship of Poets Trophy Award: "Early A.M.

Hal Grutzmacher Poetry Contest: "At the Jordan Street Café," 1st Place, "Slipstream," Honorable Mention.

2012 Press 53 Open Awards: "At the Cemetery in Green Bay," "At the Sunny Ridge Retirement Center," "A Khmer's Scarf of One Thousand Functions," Second Prize.

2013 Press 53 Open Awards: "Radium Girls," "Decoding My Mother's Ledger," "That Space We Share," Second Prize.

In a Country None of Us Called Home

But for Now I Lie Beside You

Slipstream

Yesterday you asked if our life would change
because of your heart attack.
I grabbed the sheet of air between us
and gave it a good shake
to make a commotion,
jump-starting the *no* that roared from my throat,
poured off the walls of our house.

Today I can't seem to finish anything,
my trail littered with little piles of intentions.
I could blame it on what I dreamed last night—
you know how in a dream
you need to talk to someone
and that person's always out of reach,
just leaving? If you do go before me

I will give away your empty shoes,
walk the dogs until we're all exhausted,
buy half a bag of groceries.
But for now I lie beside you, listen
to you breathe each breath, hitchhike
a ride with them into our future.

Living with Hephaestus

Some say we attract
our nightmares,
like now, when I know
my husband is about to lift
part of a sculpture
weighing one hundred pounds.

Absurd to cheer him on
when I see what it takes
to create the shapes
blazing his mind.
Day after day, sparks
cascade around him
until the image behind his eyes
bends to a form I can touch.

I don't know if it's watching
the hoist lift and swing
great sheets of steel over his head,
or if it's the fire I fear most.
The time he walked through our door
face black, holes burned
through the three layers of clothing
his leather apron didn't shield
when they caught the live end
of the welding torch.

He lowers his helmet
and strikes an arc.
Don't look, he warns,
it can blind you.
A piece of sun tears loose
and the flame hisses
hunting for contact.

That Space We Share

I love it out here on the pier,
passing the binoculars
between us, the glow from town
floating just below a moon
so close I swear I see the footprint.

As earth sails across its surface
I grab the arms of my chair,
hang on. The lunar seas glow
and we are inside the negative—
trees, water, your face etched
in copper from the bent light,
the night so still, even the waves
stop lapping. In ancient China,

men leapt, banged gongs, flashed
mirrors, shot arrows at the sky
to scare away the dragon
devouring their light.
And it was on a Greek night
much like this, when the moon
veiled her limb in earth's umbra,
Aristotle claimed our planet round.

Caught inside this glitch of time,
heads tipped back, eyes wide,
we rotate on our lawn chairs
through the spheres. The tide
bulges, pulls us into its rhythm
down the millenniums,
leaping, waving our torches,
pounding our drums.

Early A.M.

I never said
you had to love me back.
I've played the good-time reel
so many times
it's like we were always.
In sleep your arm
anchors me close
and I want to whisper
"don't move"
or you'll tear me open
and I'll leak onto the sheets,
parts of me left
in a small town
I can't even name.

Sometimes It Is Easier to Meet a Person in the Dark

On the rock, we tuck into ourselves,
breath murmuring in tight circles,
chin against knees, our palms
hugging elbows like knobby treasures.
Your shoulders are mountains
and I lean, my eyes tracking a satellite.

Somewhere, others look up.
They wear red cloth shoes, speak
sentences in flowing murals.
Beneath the night, bats loop
around their shadows. Trees
move closer and we all watch.
Even the satellite pauses.

Over Slick Rock Mountain

Bolts walk the dark on electric fingers.
The windows shudder.
Life has been good, but these days
fear crawls close to our walls.
Barbed wire right next door
where three Rottweilers in coats
of mist patrol against coyotes, cougars,
whatever sniffs and licks its lips.

This must be what war looks like
coming at you. When the unthinkable
begins, haven't people always filled
their arms, carts, carriages, cars
with what they couldn't leave?

Who's to say what I'll grab first
when the sirens wail? You of course,
the dog, cats, books, paintings,
sculptures, stones collected
from the trail we walk each day.
Oh, forget the stones, throw in

the whale rock, the moss-coated
boulders, and the one that juts
like the nose of a jet. The huge rock
layered like a novel with granite pages
and that outcrop forming the cave
we think a bear calls home. Bring
the bear, he can carry the hemlocks,
rhododendron and Buckhorn Creek.

You remind me that what we leave behind
comes along anyway, enters our thoughts
when least expected, slow like an ember,
or in a flash like the explosions buckling
the air right now. Above us, and here
is what seems odd, Orion braces
in clear splendor, as if for a last stand.

Celestial Sailor

20 x 16 x 4-foot steel sculpture

Dan and I slide back the doors
of the old barn. The heat exhales
its trapped breath across fields
that sprawl as if they had all the space
in the world. Here, where there
is nothing but blue sky and cicadas
strumming the foxtail, where oak

and ash toss their light
over the tin roof, he welds
steel into nautical shapes
and compass points,
trims sails so they can run with the wind,
while I wait for the grass
to rise and fold in our wake.

After the Argument

The phone begins its ruckus
telling me I left it
off the hook
which is what I do to escape
this jail of bones heavy
with the world
wailing on my back.
Out the door down
County Q
flooring my feet to a road
wide open headed
toward a full moon
the color of a sign
shouting *yield,*
I roar
right through grab
lunar gold before
the cedars
reach it, feet pushing
the road back
out of my way.

After I Played Tic-Tac-Toe with a Chicken

Walking down the midway
you keep reaching for my hand
but something about the carnival
makes me want to not hang on.
Pinwheels circle the night
like after the gong on New Year's Eve.
I am the electric lady.

Inside the house of mirrors
our smiles join, rows and rows
of Cheshire teeth
connecting hysterical howls.
My stomach out, yours so far back
it's inside the person
behind you.

On the carousel, my horse
wears red and yellow roses.
I wrap my fingers
around the pole.
Cotton candy sticks to my face
and I can't close my eyes.

Popcorn, screams
from the Astro Roller Coaster.
We gallop through calliope steam
toward the tattooed lady
with a map of Spain on her thigh,
you to Madrid, me straight
for Barcelona.

Trigger

Looks like a great send-off
at the table next to ours.
Grandma's ashes in a varnished box
beside a vodka martini
she took with a twist,
we hear them say.

Saved a forest from developers,
fly-fished in the Yukon, cruised
the Nile, Amazon and Ganges.
At seventy, straddled a hay bale
on her porch after hip surgery
to limber up for a camel ride
across the Gobi and sleep in a yurt.
A good death, they call it.

A good death, you echo
watching them leave, *one
with closure*. I laugh, lean
back, relish the razzmatazz buzz,
savory smells and tin ceiling,
then see from your expression
you've left this room. Back

to a war I once thought behind us
where the memories hot-wire
your nightmares. Corpses,
villages clotted with smoke.
Friends blown apart, leaving you
to shoulder their story.

We were in a patrol boat, you whisper.
The children swam toward us.
We never dreamed…we thought
they were waving.

Leaving

Let us pretend
it is morning,
that the lake's
quiet silk
is unfolding
as the sun
hooks a leg
over the first
stony ledge.
Come
before anyone else
is awake.
Disguised in gull feathers
and milkweed
we will cross
the rope bridge,
our eyes
painted with fire.

Decoding My Mother's Ledger

Figuring Out Great-Grandmother Charlotte from Nothing but a Photograph

She must have been born sometime
between the reign of The Iron Chancellor
and Lincoln's assassination, when reinforced concrete,
pasteurization and dynamite were invented.
Waving goodbye to Germany
she sailed west into her new life.

She married the year Edison turned on a light bulb.
Raised eight children while the Sioux
fought Custer at Little Big Horn,
Stanley explored the River Congo,
Tolstoy wrote *War and Peace*
and Van Gogh painted sunflowers.

In the picture, I'd swear she's holding back a smile.
Perhaps someone just told her Pankhurst
is rallying women for the vote, that they're on the move.
But for now, she wears a brooch
with her husband's likeness pinned at her throat
and she will die, possibly as the Titanic sinks,
World War 1 begins, and the atom splits.

Decoding My Mother's Ledger from July 20, 1940

Sheboygan, Wisconsin

It had to be a Saturday, Dad
loading the Packard for next week's
sales run before headed
to the Elks Lodge, its smoky rooms
the perfect spot for gin rummy,
a pitcher of beer, the news:

fire pouring from the Spitfires
and Heinkels in the Battle of Britain,
yellow stars swallowed in clusters
by German and Polish
black holes, while Mother

wheels me in white wicker
around Twelfth Street, stops
at Schmidler Drugs, Gustav's
Butcher Shop, our lives nearly normal.
The carnival comes to town.

Long wands of light scour the sky,
pull people from porch swings
and couches. The calliope's whistle
pulses the leaves of chestnuts
and elms like a callithumpian band.

Men in fedoras wait on the midway
for chances with an air gun
to knock down ducks that pop
back up, drop, and just keep coming.
In the fun house, families

stumble across tilted floors, careen
twisted slides, spinning barrels.
Midgets, snake charmers, a tattooed
king with continents stitched
to his skin. He flexes his muscles,
countries rise and fall.

Shelling

in memory of Eleanor

She saves the broken ones,
the ones with sunsets
caught between cracked lips.
And driftwood, gull feathers,
a rock with pocks that make a face.
Amulets in purses and pockets,
on shelves and sills.
No longer able to walk the beach,
stretch out on sand, she holds
a piece of China Moon
to her nose, breathes in.

The Ballerina at Ninety

If you walk
in waltz time
you won't limp,
she instructs.
I fall in meter
beside her,
my own hitch
vanishing.
Her poodle
leads the way
and we hit
the pavement
with a one,
two, three step.
Lifting her cane
she sings,
Take It To The Limit
to a tempo
the Eagles
never dreamed.

Sunday Morning with the Crystal Eagles

A choir belts out hallelujahs.
Mom's turned up the volume

on the television. This isn't an easy
story and I'll try to be clear.

She's in her rocking chair, walker
close by, afghan and Bible on her lap,

singing along with hymns so pumped
with radiance they gild the plaques

and crystal sculptures of eagles
that arrive each time she writes

the church a check.
She's well along on her pilgrim's path,

slippered feet tangled in silvered sins,
eyes fixed on sparkling mansions.

I don my cape of lilies and lambs to spend
the next hour with an evangelist in coiffed carapace,

listen as he launches his pitch in a cathedral
of stained-glass saints armed with halos.

Paranormal

I didn't ask for this—crystals, bells,
stars, tarot cards, moons, thumps
in the attic when no one is there, auras—
the whole human race parading
about wearing diaphanous bonnets.

It's a burden—doors closing, rockers
rocking. I hold life time tickets to a front
row seat in someone else's fantasy
or nightmare, their last act racing
through my mind as the curtain lifts.

Mother's dead a year, but stays in touch.
This morning the ceiling fan she never
liked stopped, reversed direction. Last week
I was baking her recipe for key lime pie
when the bulb in the oven exploded.

I burn candles, incense, tell myself
the Emeraude by Coty I smell
she never wore,
the face in the flame isn't hers.

The Bonsai, a Gift from My Children

I home in on the azalea
like a raptor, hover
over new growth, talons
sleeved in canvas.

My burden is heavy,
my back pummeled
with fat drops
of a mother's obligation.

How many times
must I pinch, prune,
wire down root ball
and branches,

bend them to the will
of my shears
before purpose twists
to pale memory?

At the Cemetery in Green Bay

I never knew where my son went
when he was supposed to be at North High.
Now he's dead
and I still can't find him.

I was just here a week ago
but I can't remember which tree,
trash can or water spigot he's near.

I've driven past lambs, angels, obelisks
and acres of graves—granite
two feet by three—just like his.

This place changes constantly.
Every time someone dies
it seems they add a gravel road.

I let Lou out of the car.
Dogs sense things.
After all she's a hound
and he had her five years.

We're the only ones alive
this morning. Lou with her nose
to the ground, tail wagging.
Me carrying a pail of pansies, sweet
alyssum and a trowel.

After Seeing *The Wizard of Oz* with Cecelia

Sudsing our hands at the old sink
in the restroom of the Majestic Theatre,
she asks if North Carolina is safe,
are the mountains strong
enough to hold back tornadoes.
She is six, anxious about twisters

and a wicked witch on the hunt
for ruby shoes,
like the ones
she is wearing.
No mention
of yesterday's
Code Black lock-
down drill
at Brevard Elementary,

when the power snapped off,
even the light in the glass aquarium
with its guppies and lone angel fish.
Her class whisked into a lavatory,
their teacher guarding the door
against the day gunshots

and chaos prowl the halls.
Much easier to worry about a turbid
sky straight out of Kansas.
Tornadoes don't happen in the mountains
that often, I say, a failed
slippery response

we both watch slide with the soap
down the enamel sides.
I look at her feet on tiptoes
so she can reach the sink,
the lace-edged socks
in those magical shoes.

Finding the Blue Ghost Fireflies

for Aleen

A stained glass window
floats outside its frame,
blossoms of pure light
bobbing low around the oak,
the laurel, my knees.
How many more
late Mays do I have left
to watch earth unclench
her leaf-matted fist
releasing this radiance?

In Willie's There's a Stool for Everyone

In Willie's There's a Stool for Everyone

It's an escape, of course, from the gray days that step back
into night at 4 p.m. The kind of day that appears next morning
in a halfhearted attempt to put out the mercury-vapor lamp
in Willie's parking lot. The old timers arrive early to watch reruns
of Mr. Ed and drink Manhattans. If you are new and order
a Pabst or a Miller, Willie always gives you a Bud.

Summer Friday night specials are frog legs or perch and Char's
cherry muffins. Everyone talks baseball and Willie shows his batting form
with an autographed Pete Rose Louisville slugger he keeps behind the bar.
But from November to May, it's burgers and fries. With leaves
off the trees you can see water through the window—right above the photo
of Willie with Whitey Herzog, the bottles of Christian Brothers and Gordons.

Tugboats like the Jimmy L. push past, their thick rubber noses
against thousand footers headed in for the winter.
The Gantry crane bends its long neck over an ore boat from Thunder Bay
while men with welding torches crawl over her.
On the stool near the jukebox Willie keeps unplugged, Butch remembers
working in temperatures thirty below, newspaper stuffed in his boots,
his fingers so cold he couldn't feel the sparks.

But Ray argues his job was worse. A night watchman,
he prowled through the empty hulls of docked freighters,
his flashlight probing boiler and bow thruster, stokehold and stanchion.
He tells how a ship groaned, twisted in the current, her bow
wrenched one way, stern another, as if giant hands
were wringing her dry. And he couldn't turn back, he says—there were clocks
to punch along the way to prove he'd walked the route.

By the end of March, we're talking Florida, Jamaica, the Bahamas,
even though we know we're going nowhere. Flo wants to make a burnt
offering of the blue gills and crappies we caught through the ice,
to hurl mittens, ice shanties, boots and snowmobiles into the fire.
Surrounded by dark paneled walls lined with glass cases—Willie's collection
of Cardinal memorabilia—we want to go to a game,
any game, sit in bleachers under the sun, and watch the Institute Cubs
play the Washington Island Islanders, our billed caps off.

Picking Up Litter Along Buck Forest Road

I don't go near the rusted car bits
crushed into two ruts, or the cross
in front of the laurel where a slick
racing tire and red bandana
hang from its arms.

Today another cross anchored
to the ground with rocks circled
by a patch of plastic petunias.
Someone's final moment fixed
to that exact spot.

I'm not related, never met
the two men killed careening
down the asphalt years apart,
silver sheets of rain hydroplaning
their cars near the place
I call home.

I don't mind the spirits of strangers
wandering the forest. God knows
these ancient mountains have burned
and broken countless backs,
their granite sides painted with waves
of stopped breath.

But I'd like to learn a bit about them
so when we meet in that space
the other side of air they'll lead me
to the crevices where the rare green
salamanders live, show me

how to find the cougar,
that long tawny stream, that leapt
across my trail just last month,
the one I was told hadn't lived
here for years.

At the Jordan Street Café

I didn't know who she was and I don't
know who asked her, but suddenly
this woman standing at the restaurant door

about ready to leave in raincoat and boots
was singing Puccini's "Vissi D'arte" from *Tosca*.
Someone turned off the CD player

and we all listened as Tosca's torment
for her dead lover took flight. Questions
to the God she felt had left her soared

over tables and bar stools, cruised down a hall
to the kitchen where even the chef paused.
It didn't matter we couldn't speak Italian,

each heart knew its own breaking,
every face translated its grief.
The aria froze us like a tableau—forks

in midair, a waiter with full tray held high,
the bartender in front of the mirrored wall
of bottles and glass about to pour a draft.

Everyone heard her music.
Some from cages. Some winged.
Some tethered to a fire, to ropes of ash.

Mel

My neighbor keeps a Christmas tree
on top of his TV fifty-two weeks a year.
Fake branches sprout glass candles
filled with colored water.
When it's plugged in, red, blue and gold
burble toward pointy tips. He claims

it's the only thing in his house with pizzazz,
that his tree has more kicks than Vegas.
Talks about the time he took the red-eye
and lost two bucks to a one-armed bandit
in the airport men's room before he even hit
The Strip. Ninety-six, a mind that leaps

from turnips to tits, he spends each day
in a La-Z-Boy facing the Motorola, flowered
afghan covering his legs, doilies under his arms
and head. Minnie, dead for twenty years,
crocheted it all. He must have worn her out,
lunging from corners, snapping her girdle,

tweaking her ass. Remorse crowds the corners
of his living room. Should've joined the Navy
instead of the Coast Guard, raised avocados
in Fallbrook and not moved to Memphis,
wishes he could erase the silence
he heard the last time he swore at his son.

Rental House—Fully Furnished

I love you, J. K. Rowling,
for pulling me inside your pages
away from these dark paneled rooms
where a two-handled bucksaw,
as long as my car, with a dangling blue
Christmas ornament shaped like a dove,
hangs five feet from the crystal chandelier.

I don't really dislike the theme
my landlord has going on the faux
marble mantelpiece—sweet grass,
a kachina doll, three pairs of antlers
and a six-inch canoe filled with bits
of dried cactus, but why
the broken chime clock
and two empty finch feeders
beside them? And I understand

about the ceramic plug-in pond
with little holes for circulating water
and the fuzzy grizzly
climbing over its plastic stones
atop the porcelain elephant end table
made in China because of course,
both animals are mammals.

Without Harry, I wouldn't be cruising
on this broom far from five upright
vacuum cleaners, three small mirrors
with *fleur-de-lis* inserts nailed
over the cat box, far,
far from a collection of porno,
six videotapes about mold
and an old mink cape draped
across a heap of Hawaiian neckties
on a barrel near the water heater
in the back hall.

Phone Call from the New Widow

My thoughts about Jim's ashes
are to go into the field on his birthday
and sprinkle a handful around the flagpole.
I think the next part of the ceremony
is to drive his ATV over the trails
and just let them blow. I'll have to figure out
what to do with everyone walking behind
since ash might fly into their faces
and that would ruin the effect.

Some I'll keep in a jar and the next time
our family goes to the cottage we'll toss
them in the water near his fishing boat.
The kids thought I was joking
when I said I'm saving half so someday
we can be mixed together, but I'm not.
His ashes were delivered by Fed Ex
in a big box. Dad's was much smaller,
about 8 by 12 inches.

Debra and Tim gave me a Fat Albert Spruce
to plant on the path to the fire pit.
They think I need a place to walk to.
I'm going to play tennis this morning,
then back to shower and meet Jackie
at the Bistro. More therapy
for my shoulder this afternoon.
I know the tennis is dumb. My rotator cuff
still hurts but I couldn't find a sub.
Maybe I just won't serve.

Boy in the White Ford Pick-Up

He pops the clutch of his grandfather's truck,
roars up and down their driveway,
from Buck Horn Road to the doublewide,
for hours at a time.

He roars up and down their driveway.
The tires howl, the radio cranked up,
for hours at a time.
With one more surge he might break free.

The air convulsed, the radio cranked up,
a late night campfire on our land,
the blaze rages to break free
over scattered Bud Light, bean, and tuna cans.

Today a fire lies cold on empty land,
paw prints circle the charred logs,
the scattered Bud Light, bean, and tuna cans.
Coyote scat, a mark of reclaimed turf.

Paw prints circle the burnt logs
the fourteen-year-old kicked aside.
Coyote scat, a mark of reclaimed turf.
But a boy can't shit to claim his space

when he messes up, feels kicked aside.
Being told to scram makes you land
where there's never enough space,
and you push at walls trying to break free.

From Buckhorn Road to the doublewide
for hours at a time
he roars up and down their driveway,
popping the clutch of his grandfather's truck.

Rescue Dog

She follows the sun around the house
as if it's her job.
The only time she moves
is when we're near,
shifting from side to back,
dusting a spot with her tail—the signal
for a belly rub we don't always give.
Hands full, too stiff
to stoop, we step over, around her,
continuing
with our day.

Her body twitches.
She cries with her muzzle closed.
I reach down to stroke the dark coat,
the old scars. I talk to her. Somewhere,
deep inside her canine brain
she races through forests and meadows
the way humans imagine
every dog must dream.
Or she's chained to a stake
with the stick coming down
again and again
and again.

Visiting a Member of the Cedar Mountain Smuckers Club (To Join You Must Be Over 90)

Did I tell you about the time
I opened the back door
and saw ten copperheads
coiled on the stoop?
It was the rain.
They were hunting
high ground.
I shook my broom,
shouted "shoo,"
and away they went.

I can show you the spring
near the state line
across from Rocky Hill
Baptist Church. In summer,
Daddy took us there to cool off.
I know I could find it.

Pansy wanted to ride Grandpa's
horse all by herself to the river.
When she got lost she let go
of the reins and old Chestnut
took her right to the still—
he knew the way sure enough.

276 used to be a two-rut road.
One summer we were coming
here from Aiken in Daddy's Ford.
We got behind a cow headed
up the mountain. Daddy drove
cow time all the way to the top.

Every August I picked berries.
Rode my horse across Buck Horn
Creek to that patch near the bald
shaped like a giant's foot.
Put up jam and syrup for days.

Mama found arrowheads on the land.
I saved them with the rattles
from the diamondbacks Jim killed.
Look, here's a boxful in case
somebody wants to display them
behind glass.

At the Mane Attraction in Brevard

I mean it's just grass, I tell Kevin,
who's painting my head
with goop from a small dish.
*Charlie shouldn't mow twice a week
in this drought. Of course it dried up.
Now he's ordered sod. Charlie,
I told him, even the Association
doesn't expect green lawns
with a moratorium on sprinkling.
Not when Fawn Lake's pulled so far
back your boat floats on stones.*

I avoid looking in the mirror,
at the gray and white strands poking
through foil squares. *Charlie needs
to relax, let nature take its course.
Enjoy the clover, dandelions, chickweed,
whatever rises to toss and blow in hot wind.
Over there,* I point. *See the mass
of strawberry blonde tumbling down
that girl's back, the one with it caught
in the clasps of her bib overalls?
I want to look like that.*

Meltdown

In Belk's among the overflowing racks
of women's casual shorts and slacks, I shove
the chic small sizes that I love far back
to scan with studied casualness the double
digits where they hang in deep disgrace.
As Cindy Crawford I could have my pick
of leather, sharkskin or Chantilly lace
that'd hug so tight I'd smolder like a wick.
God knows I've tried to cut down on the sweets
and salt, drink lite beer and one red wine
a night, eat fish—I suddenly feel petite
and grab an eight, bypass the size fourteens.
"Give it a whirl," I tell myself and sigh.
Inside the curtained dressing room I cry.

Ice Fishing

It's cold, dark and five in the morning.
Trucks roll onto the bay loaded
with heaters, lanterns, pails of bait, jig
poles and bobbers, heading toward shanties
that squat among frozen drifts
like a village of out-houses.

It's not easy walking on ice, worse
after a light snow. Inside caribou
winter boots my toes curl and uncurl,
grope their socks for more traction.

I pass men leaning against their trucks.
They swap stories, drink coffee, set
tip-ups, check lines. My flashlight sweeps
male space and their laughter dies.

I'm walking because I will not ride
in a four-ton vehicle where five months ago
I swam and canoed. Drills tattoo the air.
The ice so thick, augers spew crystals.

My neighbor's shack is buried in melt.
It rests on skis near the shipping lane.
Inside, slush swallows my boots.
The heater in the corner makes me
nervous. Why warm a hut that sits

over ice covering fathoms of water?
Then again why have lights, blankets,
magazines and a comfortable chair?
Who could relax with what's happening
below, and close to the spot
thousand footers churn through?

I peer down the glacial scope
into unbreathable mystery, search
for a glint of gill or fin.

Water Witch

I envy her certainty,
the way she jumps
from the Dodge Ram pick-up,
sets a pail filled with branches
on the ground
and picks a stick,
her arms a tanned extension
of the forked wood.
She walks
until the stick flips,
tugs her wrists down,
bends to where
it first drank.

Adele

With her walker she looks a frail eighty-eight.
We met when I drove her home from Bi-Lo
because the cab she waited for in the store's
glassed-in entry never showed. Plus, it was pouring.
She had my name after that to pick up

groceries: three bananas, one ripe,
one medium, one green, seedless red grapes,
a net bag of Brussels sprouts from the States.
Saturday nights we'd go to Natural Foods.
I'd drive to her apartment.
She'd be waiting at the kitchen table

in her blue see-through raincoat, galoshes,
pink plastic scarf, use the toilet
one more time and spritz herself with holy water
from an atomizer her priest filled each visit—
it kept her safe until she got home. Tonight

my assignment: votive candles, lavender scented
incense sticks, one bar of aloe/lime soap, two
large boxes of matches with lions on the cover.
I leave her in organic oranges, crisscross
aisles and miles of concrete, promising myself,
as I do every Saturday, this is the absolute last time.

Packing to Move to the Senior Citizens Park

Already I miss the white geranium
that refused to stop blooming,
the pot of rosemary I grew for soup.
I cannot look at what's left of the cactus

you pried off the window sill. Bits
of its branches still cling to the paint.
How can you leave your pottery?
Your kiln, wheels and clay?
The pots you loved too much to sell?

I know they are large, but I cannot do
without the lithographs of Fonteyn
and Graham. I weep for the dance—
for the dancer in those mirrors and windows

on the second floor nested in a canopy
of maple and oak. When I danced
in that forest, I was Giselle.

Friday Night at Mike's

Walter, never without a tie,
sits on the stool beside Vera.
Paula, theatrically retro in a Stetson
and sequined jean jumpsuit,
is next to Oatmeal, his dreadlocks
caught back with a piece of string.
Bicyclists, hikers, a few tourists,
the usual Friday night crowd.

The Pisgah Pickers are setting up.
High in one corner a TV on mute
pans a bombed-out market in Baghdad.
A man I've never seen before
comes in, announces he's waiting for a friend
celebrating her new role as a U.S. citizen,
and do any of us know all the words
to "God Bless America"?

One of the Pickers plucks his guitar.
Darleen, who's been here for hours,
sings a boozy...*land that I love.*
We join in, a rag tag reflection
in the mirror behind the bar.
Vera says the way the world is going to hell
it's our duty to remember.

But there's one spot where everyone hums.

At the Sunny Ridge Retirement Center

During Harriet's memorial service,
Frances leaned, put her head
on my shoulder and died—quietly

as if she didn't want to interrupt
Harriet's program.
The minister didn't see us,

no one knew except me. At the piano,
Mary played the introduction
to *Going Home.* Everyone thumbed

their hymnals for page two hundred forty-three.
I didn't know what to do, since Frances
still looked like Frances, only not quite

and she was ninety-five. I put my arm
around her so she wouldn't fall
and waited for someone to notice.

Through the French doors
finches squabbled at the bird feeder.
The squirrel we call Rocky

contemplated his next move.
A laundry truck rolled by.
I looked down at Frances' navy blue crocs,

the ones she claimed felt so much
like bedroom slippers
she could wear them anywhere.

After Attending an Exhibit of Henry Moore's Drawings and Sculpture

His life a never ending Rorschach.
Seeing the space around form,
watching it sharpen from negative into positive
until the world turns inside out
and time displaces the air with bronze.

Ideas flow from his mind in three dimensions
finding figures in a halo of motor oil, in the patterns
left by Cabernet and coffee stains,
the rhythms and angles of rhino, whale and raven.
In the margins drawn by tea leaves
or leaves in the park.

We walk home from the gallery.
Leon's on the corner in his wheelchair
waving to everyone who passes.

I look at the folds in his red plaid blanket,
see seven brothers diving from a cliff
at the same time. Nothing plaid
or wooly about them, just a lap
poured from the crucible of possibility
exploding into wings
on the hem of Leon's world.

At the Sweet Hollow Baptist Church

Pastor Harker predicts
the only way
to reach paradise
is to look straight ahead,
do not wobble.
There's a mansion
with your name engraved
right up there. Miracles
lined with fire
roll from his tongue.

Mary Alice wants so hard
to believe, she reads
the New Testament
front to back, sticks the symbol
of a fish on her old Dodge,
buys a gold cross and chain
from the antique store
in town to wear around
her neck so everyone
knows whose side she's on.

Flight #1305, Raleigh to Miami

The Stewardess.
After she's talked about seat buckles, oxygen
masks, flotation devices and emergency
lighting, she pauses, then asks if the person
who took her *People* magazine would please
return it since it was on a seat with her purse.
For a stewardess, magazines are gold.
No one confesses, even after she half jokes
the pilot will circle until she gets it back.

Seat 11 C.
Across the aisle from me, it's easy to see
she's afraid, shaky hands stuffing a carry-on bag
that's never going to fit in the overhead bin
no matter how hard she shoves. She yanks
the blind down and pulls out a battery-operated game
before the plane leaves the gate. How brave
we both are, certain we're about to explode
in fiery ether, she tapping at a palm-sized screen,
me with a pencil aimed at Dell's Cryptograms.

Seat 10 C.
I know him. Early twenties, hair combed, white
shirt, black suit, black shoes and tie. For years
he's knocked at my door no matter where I live.
Armed with a Portuguese dictionary and The Book,
he's headed for Rio, convinced that the mud roads
and steep inclines of the *favelas* will lead him
to those who haven't heard, that people will fling
their corrugated tin doors wide to welcome his story.

Seat 11 A.
She's been redoing her makeup since Raleigh,
peering into a tiny mirror to fix her expression
as it flies away from twenty-years of citizenship
and too many jobs without benefits.
Tells me she left her teenage daughter
to make it on her own. Headed back to Bogotá
and a dying mother she once knew,
ribbons of Revlon unraveling her face.

In a Country None of Us Called Home

In a Country None of Us Called Home

I don't remember what city
we were in. Barbara and I ate
something in a restaurant
I can't name, sat at a table
near two women we'd never met,
then saw again later
at a play I don't recall.
I'm uncertain how it happened
we left the crowded theatre
beside them, the four of us bunched
on a corner fanning for a cab.

Then the one in a striped dress
put two fingers into her mouth
and shrilled a piercer, the kind
that cuts street lamps in two.
It turned out we wanted
the same hotel and shared the ride.
Barbara asked her to teach us
how to whistle. Knee to knee,
the way you sometimes wish everyone
in the world could sit, our mouths
wide open, we laughed like old friends,
chins and fingers wet with spit.

Messages

Somewhere between
the gypsies campsite
and Istanbul, the bus stops.
A woman boards, leans
across my lap to wave
a paisley scarf
out the window towards
a concrete block building
set with a thousand windows.
The apartment rises
from a field of scrub grass
and litter. In the center,
up at least fifteen stories,
a hand wags a bed sheet.
The woman laughs, pumps
her small answer, keeps
on pumping.

Moscow, 1975

We rode in the back of the bus,
hands wrapped around a pole
beneath the light of one dim bulb,
swallowed by people in thick coats,
three, maybe five getting on per stop.
No one leaving. I sat on the woolen
shoulder of a man in an aisle seat.
Your ass was caught between the doors
until someone gave you a yank.

For an hour we inched down a street
where the only face I recognized
was Lenin's. You were long gone
behind body smells, diesel
and a language falling from icons.
When you called, everyone turned
as if they smelled hamburgers grilling
in the aisle. I shoved aside string bags
filled with loaves of bread and vodka,
leapt out shouting your name.

The Tooth

Killing Fields, Cambodia

Amidst ulnas, ribs,
knuckles, it rises from red
dirt after the rain.

Enamel snares sun.
Refuses to stop gleaming.
Piece of someone's smile.

56

A Khmer's Scarf of One Thousand Functions

Woven with essence of heat,
rain, fumes of red dust, trace
of jasmine, it rests on her shoulders
like the arm of a friend.

Shade from the sun, sling for the baby,
sash, towel, swatter of bugs, buffer
on her head for heavy loads,
ballooning as she turns her back.

Four corners tied, it carries taro,
rice and dragonfruit. If the wind slips
between, loose around her head,
it flares and sways like a cobra.

She buries her lips, her nose in its folds.
Silk threads cover countless questions
about the corruption she sees, filter
her words a spy must never hear.

The Village

Japan, March 12, 2011

Follow the fire
that floats
down a river
born yesterday.
Grab fistfuls
of flame.
Light
the lanterns
cold
in their eyes.

Radium Girls, 1924

Radium Dial Plant, Ottawa, Illinois

The tips of their tongues moistened
the brushes that daubed the dials
of clocks with a glow they thought
would last forever, but
it was the same as any comet's
kiss, too close, too long. They painted
their nails and skin with its salts,
combed their hair, brushed their teeth
with it for that razz-ma-tazz look.
Young and ready to shine,
they sipped phosphorous cocktails,
danced the Charleston, the shimmy
in shadowed nightclubs until dawn.
Wrapped in pure energy they glowed,
most beautiful in the dark.

On the Channel Linking Green Bay to Lake Michigan

November, 1676

Sturgeon Bay froze while the priest and guide slept.
Trapped on an island, they waited three full moons
for the ice to build. They cut oak runners
strapped them to their canoe, bound stretched leather

to make a sail. The sun rose. The ice flared.
The trees leaned south. The Potawatami guide
turned his face away from the land he knew
and pulled his wolf cloak close, drawing strength

from its animal essence. The priest stood,
flung his arms wide, black robe lifting like wings
of some sacred bird. He prayed to his god
and every saint he knew to speed them down

their frozen view. When the wind failed, they yoked
themselves with rope, pulled like a team whipped by hope.

When the Music Switches to a Minor Key

Mary Alice Tries to Save the World

She is down at the barn shoveling
manure, happy to take a break and talk.
This morning she must find two lab pups
a home, a sign at the post office says their owner
lost his job, his house is in foreclosure,
they're headed for the pound.

She dreams of saving children who ride
in wheelchairs and coaster wagons
through hospital hallways on a filament
of hope, spreads her arms to stave off attacks
on whales, wolves, pandas, polar bears,
big-eared bats, plus a litany of organisms
she can't remember.

She signs petitions. Small checks.
Letters-to-the-editor. Still her mailbox
wails with despair. She feeds her horses,
imagines slums and tent cities filled
with what the people need: goats, chickens,
wells that never run dry, gardens with dirt
so rich its blackness clings to the hoe.

County Mowing Machines

I understand this is far down the worry
chart, but every summer they grind
our roadsides, their scythes cutting
no mercy—laurel, sassafras, silverbell,
pepperbush, flame azalea. I try
to ignore them, play my guitar.
They hack through the strings. Litter
pick-up is tough; cans ground
deep into the dirt, broken bottles,
shredded Styrofoam and plastic cups.

One year I parked the Toyota along
the edge of our front yard, added bicycles,
a coaster wagon, lawn chairs and one bench.
I even considered a sit-in. The drivers
raised the blades, drove around and flattened
our mailbox—morning glories and all.

I know it's a job, but couldn't they seed
instead? Or help keep the roadsides clean?
I'm afraid that someday the plants
will simply quit their business of growing
and we'll be forced to hire the New York
Philharmonic, Mormon Tabernacle Choir,
a laser light show—whatever it takes
to bring them back before we forget
their colors, shapes, smells—their names.

Listening to a Book on Tape While Driving

Of course I can't do anything but turn it off
or listen to it, which is really no choice
at all because I've been hooked
since page one. A woman, pure evil,
I'm sure of it, pulls the strings
of three others, making their lives such hell
I want to stomp the brake and shout
look out! Or floor the accelerator, putting
miles between me and their misery.

Instead, I hurtle past acres of bucolic
scenery straight into frustration, fighting
the urge to protect the three innocents,
to call for cherubim with flaming swords,
slash a large red X on the forehead
of the she-snake so they see what I see.

I'm afraid of the ending.
The serpent always seems to win.
The wounded never get a second chance,
their gentle eyes round with surprise
like deer left to die at the side of the road.

It's a burden to be soft, like seeing
everything backward. I go to the movies
with a friend who heads for the restroom
when the music switches to a minor key
and everyone else leans forward.
If a woman's being battered
on TV, he's the one who leaves
to make the popcorn, rattling
the kernels over her screams.

I doubt if this planet can take much
more pain. Already it's spinning

out of control, wobbling on it's axis
like a punch drunk fighter trying to stay
on his feet for the count. If we could return
to that day when everything was new,
I'd rewrite the story, defang the snake, sew
a light skin of armor on the easily bruised.

Driving Back from Mt. Holy Cross

On the radio, a voice begs us to drop to our knees
right now—here where the sun hits the side
of that feed mill, and we will be forgiven for lying,
cheating, hungering for each other,
but I switch stations and we cruise past salvation
and a hitchhiking Cherokee in a black coat.

It's difficult to thumb a nose at God
when there's nothing but miles of Oklahoma,
easier amidst thick shadows of mountains
or inside the musty camouflage of a tent.

The Bible says that while God and Moses
talked on top of Sinai, Israel danced below.
Ours was the skewed version—six days
of nakedness above the clouds, frolicking
like calves before an unlit granite altar.

When lightning stalked Mt. Holy Cross
and stepped right over our tent
I remember the smell of wet nylon, of sweat
gluing us hip to hip and thinking

we could be melted, fossilized—discovered
in a millennium, two spines side-by-side,
finger bones just touching. Our families
would print posters of us. We'd be together
in car washes, health clubs, supermarkets,
the post office and city hall. There's something
I still haven't told you. When I backpack

with my husband, he carries a field guide,
reads to me and I fall asleep
dreaming of Andromeda, her skirt filled
with trillions of stars, each one over two-million
light years away. All of those zeroes
flared as trumpet bells, piled like scree,
jagged as the lightning cutting us in two.

Revelation

In Inglis, Florida, the mayor has declared
Satan won't be allowed into her town.
—Six O'clock News

Shutters nailed.
Doorbells, knobs, welcome mats
hauled to the dump. One thousand
giant crosses link arms
around the town's boundaries.
Vines spring up in backyard gardens
their tentacles stretching roof
to roof with spikes so sharp
they pierce and drain the sun.

She doesn't see
a shadow slide between the vines,
twin flames shifting like eyes.
Not a soul in church
recognizes the stranger
as he slips into the front pew,
pitchfork folded in breast pocket,
contralto in pure harmony
with the choir.

Things to Consider Before Building a House

Never let it be said
and said to our shame
that this place was beautiful
until we came.
　　　　　—Robert Stubbs

I'm not talking about how many bathrooms,
what type of stove, or designs for a house
the size of a hotel. I could make a case
for living off the grid or camping.
If we build, the mountain changes.

It'll have the same impact as airports,
malls and factories—just construction
on a smaller scale and a moving van
stacked with our footprint—glass, plastic,
wires, batteries, insulation, cleaning supplies.

Already it's a countdown for the fox, cougar,
box turtle, the trailing arbutus calling
this home. Bears and bobcats don't bother me,
but copperheads? I doubt we'll co-exist.

And of course we'll disrupt the silent
explosions of buckberry and blue erupting
between granite cracks. Gutter runoff
will scar the rock. No dusk to dawn lights
but porch lights still dim the stars.

We unroll our house plans, summon
dump trucks, bulldozers and cement
mixers as if we were gods. An omnipotent
snap of our fingers
and the mountain steps back.

A Very Small Disaster in the Scheme of Things

I put the potting soil
in the shed, don't see
the dark wings folded
like an envelope
above me, shut the door,
think it stuck, push
hard, ready to get on
with my to-do list.

But I cannot ignore I am part
of one more mammal's
slide toward extinction, so
I find the spade and pull out
a prayer from childhood.
Long after I've buried it
the last hiss sounds,
a wound in my ear.

Smoke Drinkers in Sri Lanka

The men set fire
to harvested rice paddies
preparing them for new plants.
Overhead, the birds roil.
Beaks open, they dive
through ash and boiling
red clouds, sift for insects
rising from their pyre.
You could call them by
a scientific name
to make this bird act
seem more significant
which it won't be,
since they will always
wake at dawn,
fly to burning fields
and sleep at night
wrapped in wings
the color of tropical seas.

Instructions on Divination at the Old Cemetery

Grasp the ends
of these coat hangers
I cobbled into a V.
Walk to that oak tree
covered with lichen and moss.
They say brothers
were buried beneath it
in 1865. Watch the tip
dip North, then South.
And those stones.
While Confederate forces
shelled Fort Sumter,
a father buried four
of his children here, dead
from diphtheria.
See the dents in the dirt
where he knelt,
covered with a shatter
of leaves.

Exodus

The lake rose to record highs.
Beaches disappeared, limestone bluffs eroded.
Tugs pushed barges loaded with boulders
past our house. Dump trucks paralleled them
on Highways 42 and 57. Giant cranes
and bulldozers shoveled rock into Lake Michigan's
belly, collared the shoreline with riprap.

The lake swallowed, kept climbing.
Rumors accused tough winters, wet springs,
too much messing with the environment.
God's wrath was blamed, and a nebulous person
in charge of the locks up in Sault-Ste-Marie.
Someone joked we needed Moses who'd stretched
out his arm before in a slippery situation.

Then the level started to drop—more each year.
For a while it was perfect—just the way we
thought it should be. It kept retreating.
Shorelines folded back on themselves. Naked piers
grew taller. Harbors only dreamed of boats.
Ducks napped on logs we'd never seen before.

Tourism pounded its thirsty fist. Dredgers
clawed the lake's sandy bottom. Steel jaws
dripped fossils, minnows, tiny crabs.
The water receded until bass and walleye swam
in gulches known only to the skeletons of ships.

Today I walk along a shore, last year under water.
Anemone sprout among cracked zebra mussels,

dried mossy stones. I imagine Israel's
long-ago children—how they stepped
into that split of sea as walls of water roared,

curled above their heads. I picture them stumbling
over surprised fish, the wheels of their carts
and wagons catching on coral, sinking in sediment.
How it would feel to lift an arm and stem the tide.
To change the world.

In a Country None of Us Called Home is PEG BRESNAHAN's second
collection of poetry. Her work has been published in numerous
literary journals and anthologies. She graduated from the
University of Wisconsin-Milwaukee and received her MFA in
poetry from Vermont College of Fine Arts in Montpelier. She
moved to the mountains of Western North Carolina and the
land of waterfalls from the Door County Peninsula of
Wisconsin, exchanging what she thinks of as the horizontal
water of Lake Michigan for water that is decidedly vertical.
She is a past board member of the Friends of DuPont Forest
where she lives next to DuPont State Recreational Forest in
Cedar Mountain with her husband, sculptor Dan Bresnahan,
their dog and two cats.

CPSIA information can be obtained at www.ICGtesting.com
Printed in the USA
BVOW01s1503300414

352169BV00004B/66/P